IDENTITY IN CHRIST

100 SCRIPTURES *and* AFFIRMATIONS TO BUILD CONFIDENCE

SALLIE DAWKINS

Identity in Christ: 100 Scriptures and Affirmations to Build Confidence

Copyright © 2023 by Sallie Dawkins
All Rights Reserved.

Library of Congress Control Number: 2023913206
ISBN: 978-1-955861-52-6 Print Paperback

Although the author and publisher have made every effort to ensure this book's information was correct at press time, they do not assume and hereby disclaim any liability to any party for any loss, damage, or disruption caused by errors or omissions. The information in this book does not replace or substitute professional advice in financial, medical, psychological, or legal matters.

All scripture quotations are from King James Version (KJV), public domain, sourced from www.BibleGateway.com.

Published by
Firebrand United LLC
216 Skywatch Drive #206
Danville, Kentucky
40422 USA
www.FirebrandUnited.com

CONTENTS

How to Use This Resource 5

Old Testament Scriptures 8

New Testament Scriptures 34

Do You Know Jesus? 112

Can You Help? 114

More from this Publisher 115

How to Use This Resource

When we ask Jesus to be our Savior and Lord, we begin our eternal journey of discovering who God is.

Our God is the great I Am (Exodus 3:14), and He created us in His image (Genesis 1:27). As Christians, whatever we say about God, we can say about ourselves and others. Likewise, if we wouldn't say it about God, we shouldn't say it about ourselves or others.

This foundational revelation came decades after I first became a Christian. How can we walk in His authority until we know and understand our identity in Christ? How can we "be about our Father's business" (Luke 2:49) if we don't have a personal relationship with Him or believe He is who He says He is?

Identity in Christ: 100 Scriptures and Affirmations to Build Confidence is an excellent introductory guide to identity. God talks about identity throughout the Old and New Testaments of the Bible. His Word actively declares and reveals His lovingkindness.

This book contains Bible verses about identity from the King James (KJV) translation. You'll discover a paraphrased affirmation in the box above each scripture.

Affirmations provide a way to reinforce our faith, remember God's promises, and cultivate a positive mindset rooted in God's love and grace. Affirmations are self-focused, yet appeal to many.

I encourage you to highlight these scriptures in your Bible or write them in your journal. Doing so will assist you in memorizing God's Word. Read the scriptures in your favorite translation for greater understanding. Some verses might challenge your beliefs, but others will comfort you. Focusing on scripture shifts our gaze to God.

Meditating on scripture changed my outlook on life, and I believe it will be the same for you. This guide is perfect for new Christians, street evangelism, or outreach ministry.

Reference this book's scriptures and affirmations to create faith declarations. Declarations differ from affirmations in that they're God-focused. We can easily pull scripture into our circumstances, decreeing, "God is, God can, God will, God does, or God has," all according to His Word. Declarations express faith in God's power.

I pray this book opens the door to continued conversation with God and that you grow from the experience.

Your sister in Christ,

Sallie Dawkins

P.S. I encourage you to read the Bible to discover hundreds of additional identity scriptures not included here. My book, *Complete in Christ: Discovering Identity, Provision, and Purpose within God's Word*, is a more comprehensive resource with over one thousand scriptures indexed in over one-hundred categories to help Christians discover their identity, provision, and purpose within God's Word.

Old Testament Scriptures

I am created in God's image.

So God created man in his own image, in the image of God created he him; male and female created he them. (**Genesis 1:27**)

> I am
> God's special
> creation.
> His breath
> gives me life.

And the LORD God formed man of the dust of the ground, and breathed into his nostrils the breath of life; and man became a living soul. (**Genesis 2:7**)

> I am
> holy and
> set apart
> for God.

And ye shall be holy unto me: for I the LORD am holy, and have severed you from other people, that ye should be mine. (**Leviticus 20:26**)

> I am
> blessed
> as I enter
> and blessed
> as I leave.

Blessed shalt thou be when thou comest in, and blessed shalt thou be when thou goest out. (**Deuteronomy 28:6**)

I am never alone.

And the LORD, he it is that doth go before thee; he will be with thee, he will not fail thee, neither forsake thee: fear not, neither be dismayed. (**Deuteronomy 31:8**).

> I am
> loved and
> cherished
> by the LORD.

For the LORD will not forsake his people for his great name's sake: because it hath pleased the LORD to make you his people. **(1 Samuel 12:22)**

I am crowned with glory and honor.

For thou hast made him a little lower than the angels, and hast crowned him with glory and honour. (**Psalm 8:5**)

I am
the apple
of God's eye.

Keep me as the apple of the eye, hide me under the shadow of thy wings. (**Psalm 17:8**)

> I am shielded from harm by God's grace.

Thou hast also given me the shield of thy salvation: and thy right hand hath holden me up, and thy gentleness hath made me great. (**Psalm 18:35**)

> I am
> safe and protected,
> even when faced
> with challenges.

Thou preparest a table before me in the presence of mine enemies: thou anointest my head with oil; my cup runneth over. (**Psalm 23:5**)

> I am
> blessed
> with God's
> peace.

The LORD will give strength unto his people; the LORD will bless his people with peace. (**Psalm 29:11**)

> # I am protected and loved by God.

The LORD will preserve him, and keep him alive; and he shall be blessed upon the earth: and thou wilt not deliver him unto the will of his enemies. (**Psalm 41:2**)

> I am
> kept safe
> by God.

For he shall give his angels charge over thee, to keep thee in all thy ways. (**Psalm 91:11**)

> I am part of God's special flock, and trust His guidance.

Know ye that the LORD he is God: it is he that hath made us, and not we ourselves; we are his people, and the sheep of his pasture. (**Psalm 100:3**)

> I am
> a child of God,
> saved from the
> hand of
> the enemy.

Let the redeemed of the LORD say so, whom he hath redeemed from the hand of the enemy. (**Psalm 107:2**)

I am special and unique, created with care.

I will praise thee; for I am fearfully and wonderfully made: marvellous are thy works; and that my soul knoweth right well. (**Psalm 139:14**)

> # I am beautiful in God's eyes.

Behold, thou art fair, my love; behold, thou art fair; thou hast doves' eyes. **(Song of Solomon 1:15)**

> I am redeemed and precious to God.

But now thus saith the LORD that created thee..., Fear not: for I have redeemed thee, I have called thee by thy name; thou art mine. (**Isaiah 43:1**)

> As God's
> witness,
> I am
> chosen
> and loved.

Ye are my witnesses, saith the LORD, and my servant whom I have chosen: that ye may know and believe me, and understand that I am he. (**Isaiah 43:10**)

> I am
> always in
> God's thoughts
> and care.

Behold, I have graven thee upon the palms of my hands; thy walls are continually before me. (**Isaiah 49:16**)

> I am
> filled with joy
> and praise
> the LORD
> each day.

I will greatly rejoice in the LORD, my soul shall be joyful in my God; for he hath clothed me with the garments of salvation, he hath covered me with the robe of righteousness. (**Isaiah 61:10**)

> I am
> a beautiful
> creation of love,
> crafted by our
> heavenly Father's
> skilled hands.

But now, O LORD, thou art our father; we are the clay, and thou our potter; and we all are the work of thy hand. (**Isaiah 64:8**)

> I am
> loved by the Lord,
> and His thoughts
> about me
> are full of peace
> and goodness.

For I know the thoughts that I think toward you, saith the LORD, thoughts of peace, and not of evil, to give you an expected end. (**Jeremiah 29:11**)

> I am
> drawn towards
> God's kindness
> and love.

The LORD hath appeared of old unto me, saying, Yea, I have loved thee with an everlasting love: therefore with lovingkindness have I drawn thee. **(Jeremiah 31:3)**

> # I am cherished and loved unconditionally.

And I will betroth thee unto me for ever; yea, I will betroth thee unto me in righteousness, and in judgment, and in lovingkindness, and in mercies. (**Hosea 2:19**)

New Testament Scriptures

> I am
> a child of God
> who brings peace
> and harmony
> to the world
> around me.

Blessed are the peacemakers: for they shall be called the children of God. (**Matthew 5:9**)

> I am
> God's unique child,
> adding flavor and
> goodness to the
> world.

Ye are the salt of the earth: but if the salt have lost his savour, wherewith shall it be salted. (**Matthew 5:13**)

> # I am
> # a shining light
> # in this world.

Ye are the light of the world. A city that is set on an hill cannot be hid. (**Matthew 5:14**)

> I am establishing God's Kingdom on earth.

And I will give unto thee the keys of the kingdom of heaven: and whatsoever thou shalt bind on earth shall be bound in heaven. (**Matthew 16:19**)

I am kind and humble like a little child.

Whosoever therefore shall humble himself as this little child, the same is greatest in the kingdom of heaven. (**Matthew 18:4**)

> I am
> a powerful
> messenger of love
> and healing.

And he sent them to preach the kingdom of God, and to heal the sick. (**Luke 9:2**)

> I am
> a child
> of God.

But as many as received him, to them gave the power to become the sons of God, even to them that believe on his name. (**John 1:12**)

I am born of the Spirit.

The wind bloweth where it listeth, and thou hearest the sound thereof, but canst not tell whence it cometh, and whither it goeth: so is every one that is born of the Spirit. (**John 3:8**)

> I am
> loved and
> guided
> by God's Word.

It is written in the prophets, and they shall be all taught of God. Every man therefore that hath heard, and hath learned of the Father, cometh unto me. (**John 6:45**)

I am free from all bondage.

If the Son therefore shall make you free, ye shall be free indeed. (**John 8:36**)

I am connected to a strong and loving God.

I am the vine, ye are the branches: He that abideth in me, and I in him, the same bringeth forth much fruit: for without me ye can do nothing. (**John 15:5**)

I am loved unconditionally.

As the Father hath loved me, so have I loved you: continue ye in my love. (**John 15:9**)

I am God's friend.

Henceforth I call you not servants; for the servant knoweth not what his lord doeth: but I have called you friends. (**John 15:15**)

> I am
> chosen and
> empowered
> to make a
> positive difference
> in the world.

Ye have not chosen me, but I have chosen you, and ordained you, that ye should go and bring forth fruit, and that your fruit should remain. (**John 15:16**)

I am protected from the evil one.

I pray not that thou shouldest take them out of the world, but that thou shouldest keep them from the evil. (**John 17:15**)

> I am
> filled with love
> and wisdom
> when I learn
> and live according
> to the truth
> of God's Word.

Sanctify them through thy truth: thy word is truth. (**John 17:17**)

I am one with God.

I in them, and thou in me, that they may be made perfect in one; and that the world may know that thou hast sent me, and hast loved them, as thou hast loved me. (**John 17:23**)

> Everywhere I go,
> I am
> a brave and strong
> witness of God's
> love and kindness.

But ye shall receive power, after that the Holy Ghost is come upon you: and ye shall be witnesses unto me... unto the uttermost part of the earth. (**Acts 1:8**)

> I am
> full of the
> Holy Spirit
> and faith.

For he was a good man, and full of the Holy Ghost and of faith: and much people was added unto the Lord. (**Acts 11:24**)

I am loved and forgiven.

And by him all that believe are justified from all things, from which ye could not be justified by the law of Moses. (**Acts 13:39**)

> I am
> loved and accepted
> by God because
> I have faith
> in Jesus.

Therefore being justified by faith, we have peace with God through our Lord Jesus Christ. (**Romans 5:1**)

> I am
> strong and free
> from sin,
> for my
> old self is gone.

Knowing this, that our old man is crucified with him, that the body of sin might be destroyed, that henceforth we should not serve sin. (**Romans 6:6**)

> I am
> alive in
> Christ.

Likewise reckon ye also yourselves to be dead indeed unto sin, but alive unto God through Jesus Christ our Lord. (**Romans 6:11**)

> I am
> free from sin,
> and choose
> to do what is
> right and good.

Being then made free from sin, ye became the servants of righteousness. (**Romans 6:18**)

> I am worthy and loved, for I am in Christ Jesus.

There is therefore now no condemnation to them which are in Christ Jesus, who walk not after the flesh, but after the Spirit. (**Romans 8:1**)

I am led by the Spirit of God.

For as many as are led by the Spirit of God, they are the sons of God. (**Romans 8:14**)

I am a child of God, and I call Him my loving Father.

For ye have not received the spirit of bondage again to fear; but ye have received the Spirit of adoption, whereby we cry, Abba, Father. (**Romans 8:15**)

> I am grateful for the special place I hold in God's heart.

And if children, then heirs; heirs of God, and joint-heirs with Christ; if so be that we suffer with him, that we may be also glorified together. (**Romans 8:17**)

> # I am destined for greatness and called to be amazing.

Moreover whom he did predestinate, them he also called: and whom he called, them he also justified: and whom he justified, them he also glorified. (**Romans 8:30**)

> I can conqueror anything with Christ.

Nay, in all these things we are more than conquerors through him that loved us. (**Romans 8:37**)

> # I am accepted by God.

Wherefore receive ye one another, as Christ also received us to the glory of God. (**Romans 15:7**)

> I am
> a special temple
> of love, and
> God's Spirit lives
> inside of me!

Know ye not that ye are the temple of God, and that the Spirit of God dwelleth in you? (**1 Corinthians 3:16**)

> I am
> united
> with God
> as one spirit.

But he that is joined unto the Lord is one spirit. (**1 Corinthians 6:17**)

I am a member of the body of Christ.

Now ye are the body of Christ, and members in particular. (**1 Corinthians 12:27**)

I am fully known by God.

For now we see through a glass, darkly; but then face to face: now I know in part; but then shall I know even as also I am known. (**1 Corinthians 13:12**)

I am victorious through Jesus.

But thanks be to God, which giveth us the victory through our Lord Jesus Christ. (**1 Corinthians 15:57**)

> I am being transformed from within to reveal God's glory.

But we all, with open face beholding as in a glass the glory of the Lord, are changed into the same image from glory to glory, even as by the Spirit of the Lord. (**2 Corinthians 3:18**)

> I am growing in my new identity in Christ, and old things no longer define me.

Therefore if any man be in Christ, he is a new creature: old things are passed away; behold, all things are become new. **(2 Corinthians 5:17)**

> I am blessed with the power to bring peace and love to others.

And all things are of God, who hath reconciled us to himself by Jesus Christ, and hath given to us the ministry of reconciliation. (**2 Corinthians 5:18**)

> I choose
> to bring
> God's love
> to everyone
> I meet.

Now then we are ambassadors for Christ, as though God did beseech you by us: we pray you in Christ's stead, be ye reconciled to God. (**2 Corinthians 5:20**)

> # I am the righteousness of God in Christ.

For he hath made him to be sin for us, who knew no sin; that we might be made the righteousness of God in him. (**2 Corinthians 5:21**)

I am rich in God's grace.

For ye know the grace of our Lord Jesus Christ, that, though he was rich, yet for your sakes he became poor, that ye through his poverty might be rich. (**2 Corinthians 8:9**)

I am a cheerful giver.

Every man according as he purposeth in his heart, so let him give; not grudgingly, or of necessity: for God loveth a cheerful giver. (**2 Corinthians 9:7**)

I am a child of God through my faith in Christ Jesus.

For ye are all the children of God by faith in Christ Jesus. (**Galatians 3:26**)

I am blessed to inherit God's love and goodness!

Wherefore thou art no more a servant, but a son; and if a son, then an heir of God through Christ. (**Galatians 4:7**)

> # I am blessed with every spiritual blessing.

Blessed be the God and Father of our Lord Jesus Christ, who hath blessed us with all spiritual blessings in heavenly places in Christ. (**Ephesians 1:3**)

> # I am holy and blameless before God.

According as he hath chosen us in him before the foundation of the world, that we should be holy and without blame before him in love. (**Ephesians 1:4**)

I am chosen by Jesus with love and joy.

Having predestinated us unto the adoption of children by Jesus Christ to himself, according to the good pleasure of his will. (**Ephesians 1:5**)

I am forgiven of all sin.

In whom we have redemption through his blood, the forgiveness of sins, according to the riches of his grace. (**Ephesians 1:7**)

> I am sealed with the Holy Spirit of promise.

In whom ye also trusted, after that ye heard the word of truth, the gospel of your salvation: in whom also after that ye believed, ye were sealed with that holy Spirit of promise. (**Ephesians 1:13**)

I am seated in heavenly places with Christ.

And hath raised us up together, and made us sit together in heavenly places in Christ Jesus. (**Ephesians 2:6**)

> I am saved by grace through faith.

For by grace are ye saved through faith; and that not of yourselves: it is the gift of God. (**Ephesians 2:8**)

> # I am God's handiwork.

For we are his workmanship, created in Christ Jesus unto good works, which God hath before ordained that we should walk in them. (**Ephesians 2:10**)

I am part of God's family.

Now therefore ye are no more strangers and foreigners, but fellow citizens with the saints, and of the household of God. **(Ephesians 2:19)**

I am bold and confident in Christ.

In whom we have boldness and access with confidence by the faith of him. **(Ephesians 3:12)**

> I am rooted and grounded in God's love.

That Christ may dwell in your hearts by faith; that ye, being rooted and grounded in love. (**Ephesians 3:17**)

> I am
> a new man,
> created in
> the likeness
> of God.

And that ye put on the new man, which after God is created in righteousness and true holiness. (**Ephesians 4:24**)

> # I am
> # a child
> # of light.

For ye were sometimes darkness, but now are ye light in the Lord: walk as children of light. (**Ephesians 5:8**)

I am strong in the Lord.

Finally, my brethren, be strong in the Lord, and in the power of his might. (**Ephesians 6:10**)

> I am filled with Jesus' love and kindness, spreading goodness everywhere I go.

Being filled with the fruits of righteousness, which are by Jesus Christ, unto the glory and praise of God. **(Philippians 1:11)**

> I am
> a citizen
> of heaven and
> speak God's
> language of love.

For our conversation is in heaven; from whence also we look for the Saviour, the Lord Jesus Christ. (**Philippians 3:20**)

I am created to be holy and flawless.

In the body of his flesh through death, to present you holy and unblameable and unreproveable in his sight. (**Colossians 1:22**)

> I am complete in Christ.

And ye are complete in him, which is the head of all principality and power. (**Colossians 2:10**)

I am chosen by God.

Knowing, brethren beloved, your election of God. (**1 Thessalonians 1:4**)

> # I am
> # a child of light,
> # shining bright
> # with joy.

Ye are all the children of light, and the children of the day: we are not of the night, nor of darkness. (**1 Thessalonians 5:5**)

I am passionate for good works.

Who gave himself for us, that he might redeem us from all iniquity, and purify unto himself a peculiar people, zealous of good works. (**Titus 2:14**)

I am loved and protected by God.

Wherefore he is able also to save them to the uttermost that come unto God by him, seeing he ever liveth to make intercession for them. (**Hebrews 7:25**)

> # I am grateful for all I have, and choose to be content.

Let your conversation be without covetousness; and be content with such things as ye have: for he hath said, I will never leave thee, nor forsake thee. (**Hebrews 13:5**)

I am holy through Christ.

Because it is written, Be ye holy; for I am holy. (**1 Peter 1:16**)

> I am valuable and loved, for I have been saved by the precious blood of Jesus.

Forasmuch as ye know that ye were not redeemed with corruptible things... But with the precious blood of Christ, as of a lamb without blemish and without spot. (**1 Peter 1:18-19**)

> I am
> a unique and
> precious stone,
> being built up to
> become a special
> part of God's
> spiritual house.

Ye also, as lively stones, are built up a spiritual house, an holy priesthood, to offer up spiritual sacrifices, acceptable to God by Jesus Christ. (**1 Peter 2:5**)

> I am
> a chosen race,
> a royal priesthood,
> and a holy nation.

But ye are a chosen generation, a royal priesthood, an holy nation, a peculiar people; that ye should shew forth the praises of him who hath called you out of darkness into his marvellous light. (**1 Peter 2:9**)

I am strong and watchful.

Be sober, be vigilant; because your adversary the devil, as a roaring lion, walketh about, seeking whom he may devour. (**1 Peter 5:8**)

> # I have victory over darkness and evil.

Ye are of God, little children, and have overcome them: because greater is he that is in you, than he that is in the world. (**1 John 4:4**)

> # I am
> # an heir of
> # eternal life.

And this is the record, that God hath given to us eternal life, and this life is in his Son. (**1 John 5:11**)

> I am
> a child of God
> and I choose to
> do what is right.

We know that whosoever is born of God sinneth not; but he that is begotten of God keepeth himself, and that wicked one toucheth him not. (**1 John 5:18**)

> I am
> brave, strong,
> and full of love.
> I overcome
> challenges with the
> Lamb's blood and
> my own words.

And they overcame him by the blood of the Lamb, and by the word of their testimony; and they loved not their lives unto the death. (**Revelation 12:11**)

Do You Know Jesus?

Romans 10:9 tells us, "That if thou shalt confess with thy mouth the Lord Jesus, and shalt believe in thine heart that God hath raised him from the dead, thou shalt be saved."

If Jesus Christ is not yet your Savior and Lord, you can pray this prayer to invite Him into your life.

> Dear God,
>
> I acknowledge that I am a sinner and cannot save myself.
>
> I believe Jesus came to pay for my sins fully.
>
> I am sorry for my wrongdoings and ask for forgiveness.
>
> I believe Jesus is Your Son, Who died and was buried but rose again after three days, conquering death and hell.

I am grateful that I am no longer condemned to death but have received the gift of eternal life through Jesus.

I believe the blood of Jesus cleanses me and makes me whole.

By faith, I accept Your forgiveness and love.

Jesus, I invite You to be my Savior and Lord and the Holy Spirit to guide me in Your ways.

Please fill me with Your presence and power, and help me live for You.

Thank You for Your love, mercy, and grace.

In Jesus' name,

Amen.

If you've just prayed this prayer for the first time, I encourage you to connect with other believers by joining a local church. Welcome to the family of Christ!

Can You Help?

We appreciate feedback and love hearing what readers have to say. Your input helps to make subsequent versions of this book and future books better.

Please leave an honest book review. Consider sharing your favorite quote or including a photo!

Stay up-to-date with new releases by visiting www.SallieDawkins.com.

More from this Publisher

- Healing Words: 100 Scriptures and Affirmations for Wholeness
- 311 Questions Jesus Asked
- Spirit World Truths from God's Word
- God's Promises of Abundance for Healing
- Complete in Christ: Discovering Identity, Provision, and Purpose within God's Word
- God's Wisdom for Wealth: Flouring in Family & Business
- You Can Hear the Voice of God Through All Your Spiritual Senses
- You Can Know the Heart of God for Your Life
- You Can Share the Love of God with Others
- The Awakening Christian: Complete Series (Nov 2023)
- Maggie's Legacy: Lessons in Spiritual Obedience Learned from My Border Collie

Printed in Great Britain
by Amazon